What's so funny about looking for a job?

Scott Badler

CompCare® Publishers
Minneapolis, Minnesota

Library of Congress Cataloging-in-Publication Data

Badler, Scott.
    What's so funny about looking for a job?/Scott Badler
        p.cm.
ISBN 0-89638-365-2
1. Job-hunting—Humor 2. Job-hunting—Caricatures and car-
toons. I. Title. II. Title: What's so funny about looking for a job?
PN6231.J59B33 1993
818' .5402—dc20   93-24644
                                                                CIP

Text and cartoon ideas by Scott Badler
Cover design by MacLean and Tuminelly
Illustrations by Steve Michaels
Interior design by Leah Griesbach

Inquiries, orders, and catalog requests should be addressed to
CompCare Publishers
3850 Annapolis Lane, Suite 100
Minneapolis, MN 55447
Call 612/559-4800
or toll free 800/328-3330

To Mom, Dad, and my brother Randy, whose encouragement to follow my dreams has never wavered, and to those I met on my own job searches, who unwittingly provided the inspiration for this book.

I would also like to acknowledge Elaine Gottlieb, who helped to originate the idea for this book and co-authored Chapter Five, "The Twenty-four-hour-a-day Job Search."

Contents

Introduction

This book isn't about making your job search more fun. It's about helping you keep your sanity while you look for a job.

Remember that you're not the only one who may be feeling the ill effects of your job search. Your frustration, anger, and depression are probably affecting all the important people in your life—sons, daughters, wives, husbands, friends, and parents.

It's important for you to relieve the stress of job-hunting. Sometimes the stress of job-hunting and the accompanying feelings of constant rejection are so overwhelming, we take our frustration out on those we care about most. You are a person on an emotional roller coaster, a person who comes home hopeful after a promising interview, and the next day, after you weren't selected, resembles the captain on deck of the sinking Titanic.

Job loss has been associated with both physical and psychological consequences. Not only can it cause withdrawal and self-doubt, but it can introduce family strains that may lead to family conflict.

Let's face it, at times during your job search you will hit rock bottom. You didn't get a job you really wanted; you have no prospects for job leads; your unemployment insurance is running out. There will be times when you will need to relieve the stress of looking for a job. One of the best ways to do that is to laugh. Guffaw. Titter. Giggle. Chuckle.

This book may help. Read a bit or laugh with it when you're down in the dumps. Relieve, temporarily, the pressure and agony of looking for a job.

The process is extremely difficult. It's like playing a game of tennis against an opponent you can never seem to beat. You keep playing, but the score is always the same. You lose. And lose. And lose some more. Until one day, by some freak set of circumstances—an alignment of the stars or a World Series between the Chicago Cubs and the Cleveland Indians—you come out on top.

Looking for a job is like that. You have no choice but to play the game. It's sort of like playing hide-and-seek and you're always "It." Your task is to search for the ever-elusive and reclusive employer. Unfortunately, you can't call a halt when you're tired of playing.

The average job search takes six months. If the period of unemployment falls inconveniently during a recession, the hunt takes even longer. If you have ever looked for a job, are looking now, or know a friend or loved one who is seeking employment, you know how tough it can be.

When the pink slip arrives, self-esteem takes a nose-dive. Since many people base their self-worth on their profession, they take a whack to their self-esteem when unemployment occurs. Add some mounting bills, and depression can become your unwanted, but constant, companion.

I remember a time during my childhood when my own father was out of work. After looking for a few months, he became a finalist for a top position that would have paid him twice what he had been earning. When he didn't get the job, he went into an emotional slump that lasted a week.

During my father's unemployment, my mother made heroic attempts to save money. Instead of regular milk, she bought powdered milk, which I detested. I knew then how horrible it was to be unemployed. I hoped that Dad would get back to work as soon as possible.

Job-hunting is stressful, time-consuming, labor-intensive, and low-paying. Some job-seekers describe the process as an endless ride of hope and despair.

Looking for a job in today's world has become an all-encompassing project. It's a forty-hour-a-week job. But it wasn't always this hard. Some of you may remember when finding a job meant combing the Want Ads for a couple of weeks, calling some old contacts, or going to a personnel agency. Not anymore. Nowadays, the job search often lasts longer than the job itself. Looking for a job can be harder than actually *doing* the job.

Job-hunting requires you to make endless sales calls, to use sophisticated marketing techniques, to navigate your way to new destinations, to probe strangers for information, and to psych yourself up for interviews. You've got to sell yourself and quickly analyze each new situation so you can adjust your personality accordingly. Besides all that, you need to negotiate! Give me a break! Looking for work is a full-time job—with plenty of opportunities for unpaid overtime!

Final instructions: Don't take your frustrations out on those who care about you. Take them out on this book! Use it as a temporary escape from Job-Hunting Land. Use it as a release valve. Read it, abuse it, throw it against the wall, hit it with a bat. Call *it* names (not your kids) until you find a job. And, in time, you will.

Chapter One

How to Tell if You're Unemployed

The first question you need to answer is *Am I unemployed?* It's a question many people don't take the time to think through. But a wrong answer has serious repercussions.

If you are employed, you don't want to make the mistake of going to the unemployment office, filing a claim, and finding out you are a W-2-type person. Or being told by your friendly compensation specialist, "The Deekins Drug Company has informed us that you are the vice-president of sales, pharmaceutical division. You supervise three salespeople and two secretaries. You also have a 2 P.M. meeting scheduled today."

However, a reality-check visit to the House of Unemployment is never out of line. In this case, a securely employed but disgruntled employee stops by the unemployment office during a particularly difficult time at work. The purpose of his visit is to determine if waiting an hour in the unemployment line is better than being driven insane at work.

Some people get paid to do nothing. Who are these people and are they really employed? What about the consultants who pick up $60,000 a year for being related to a government official? How about board members of large companies? They attend a luncheon every couple of months, lend their names, and rake in thousands of dollars. Does that constitute work? Is this you? Probably not. Keep reading.

Another category of nonemployed workers is celebrities. They make money, but do they have jobs? Former basketball star Wilt Chamberlain says, "A celebrity can make money doing nothing these days."

Let's consider Zsa Zsa Gabor. Is she employed? Did she ever hold down a job? Is being a full-time celebrity considered a career? What's her next career move? How does she develop her skills? Has she ever been laid off?

What about the Bud Man? Does a guy who makes his living residing in six packs count as a beer-guzzling worker?

Celebrities don't count. If you're a celebrity, this book is not for you.

Questionnaire

So now you have some idea whether you need to look for a job. But you're still not sure. When in doubt, test your knowledge. Take this short quiz. You may begin.

1. Do you frequently call friends of a friend of a cousin twice removed you never heard of who used to be in a business you once had a job in?

    _____Always
    _____Never
    _____Just for Fun

2. Does the word *network* signify your favorite television company, or does it mean talking to strangers about their line of work?

3. Have you forgotten how to set your alarm clock?

4. A sexy person wearing provocative clothes and a gorgeous smile takes a seat next to you at the bar and asks you if you come here often.

   Do you . . .
   _____ shake hands and give him/her your resumé?
   _____ probe for job leads?
   _____ ask if Remington is his/her shaver of choice?
   _____ ask what color his/her parachute is?

5. When you doodle, do the drawings resemble yourself sitting in an office?

6. Do you find yourself writing more letters in one week than you have in the past decade?

7. Although you're a pacifist, does the idea of enlisting in the armed forces seem attractive simply for the regular paycheck and benefits?

8. Your teenage son announces that he has been born again.

   You respond by asking . . .
   _____ what the cost is, thinking back to the first time he was born when it set you back $1,000.
   _____ if membership includes medical benefits.
   _____ if they're hiring.

9. Do you tell your preschool-aged children that it's important for them to get job experience as soon as possible and shove them out in the neighborhood to hawk encyclopedias?

10. When a friend suggests that the two of you go hunting, do you arrive armed with resumés?

11. You're at a dinner party and the conversation turns to "shop talk."

> Do you . . .
> _____ talk about your fix-it shop in the basement?
> _____ announce "I need a shave," and turn on your cordless Remington?
> _____ knock over your bowl of soup in an attempt to change the subject?

12. Do you consider your bathrobe proper attire for any time of the day?

13. Do you find yourself altering song lyrics to reflect your number one priority and humming them in public places? Example: The Beatles' song "I Wanna Hold Your Hand" becomes "I Wanna Hold That Job."

14. Looking for a job
> _____ requires gas.
> _____ is a gas.
> _____ gives me gas.
> _____ demands a Remington Shaver.

15. Complete this question: Tomorrow I am going . . .

> _____ to look for a job.
> _____ Other

Good work. You've finished in the allotted time period. Take a breather. If you are like many of the hundreds of people who have completed this exam, you are excited and confused and dying to know some answers. How did I do? Where do I stand? What's my score? Did I win? Should I have cheated?

First of all, the test was divided into four major areas. One area included misleading or trick questions. The second included questions of no importance whatsoever. The third eased up with a couple of "gimmes," or questions only an idiot could get wrong. And the fourth included questions required under the author's pre-existing contract with the fine folks at Remington shavers.

For example, Question 9 is a gimme. Whether or not you are employed, your children should be selling encyclopedias. The income can go toward their college education, and they'll be the only kids on the block who will have experience in publishing before they've learned to read.

Question 11 is a trick question. Employed or not, it is always a good idea to knock over your bowl of soup when the conversation turns to "shop talk."

Are you getting the idea that job-hunting is a tricky business with no clear-cut answers?

To find out more about the origin of job-hunting, a likely candidate for the eighth Wonder of the World, read on.

What You Should Know about Looking for a Job

Okay, so you fit neatly into the "looking for work" category. Welcome to the club. (Would you mind being the secretary?)

Now for some basic information. If this is your first time looking for a job, you'll probably have some questions. What follows are the answers you'll need to know—even before you've asked them. Pretty good, huh? You'll have a head start on other job-hunters.

Is it legal to have sex while collecting unemployment benefits?

This is the first question unemployed people ask, fearing that, since their jobs have been taken away, sex might be next. Not to worry. Sex is one of those catch-all "inalienable rights" provided for in the Foreplay to the Constitution.

However, there are two places you should be cautious about having sex: in the unemployment line and at job interviews. Studies show this type of behavior may reduce your ability to collect benefits or decrease your shot at a second interview.

The question of whether sex is conducive to successful job-hunting is still being hotly debated. On one side are those who say sex not only clears your mind, but it also is an excellent networking tool. Opposing them is the unlikely coalition of (1) career counselors who say thinking about sex takes your mind away from the primary goal of finding work and (2) the Church, which frowns on the intimacy of sex before the sacred union of company and employee is complete.

I'm willing to relocate, but where do I look for a job?

The answer to this question is readily available on the license plates of out-of-state cars. The states have made it convenient for you by putting job information right on the license plates.

For example, thinking about a career in "vacations"? Try Maine, whose plate reads "Vacationland." This state is a lot better than Fantasyland or Disneyland's Tomorrowland, because it's bigger and has many more moose.

Don't waste your time on Wisconsin if you're kosher or have an intolerance for dairy products because you'll learn from the license plate that this is "America's Dairyland." The jobs here deal mostly with cheese and milk.

New Hampshire's plate reads "Live Free or Die," not "Live *for* Free and Die." Make sure you know what you're getting into before you move there. It is also known as "The Granite State," so don't go there unless you're a rock hound—and a good one at that.

Consider Florida, "The Sunshine State." Here you can make your living off the sun. Jobs are plentiful in lifeguarding and the removal of skin cancers.

Massachusetts is "The Spirit of America." Lots of work for cheerleaders here.

And so on. There are fifty-or-so states for you to research, as well as territories like Puerto Rico and other lands.

Yes, as strange as it may seem, you can job-hunt as you take a Sunday drive. But a word of caution: don't tailgate!

During an interview, should I tell the truth about the skeletons in my closet?

It is our understanding that you need only be truthful when you're in court and are asked to "swear to tell the truth, the whole truth, and nothing but the truth." Fibs, half-truths, and white lies are acceptable if they get you a job.

How can I make looking for a job FUN?

The best way to make job-hunting fun is to be creative. For example, imagine that you're a famous sleuth or detective. Pretend you're James Bond attempting to cut a swath through the human resources department in your effort to corner a decision-maker. "My name is Slobovitwitz," you say as you drink your stirred, not shaken, coffee. "Stanley Slobovitwitz."

Congratulate yourself on your excellent portrayal of Peter Sellers as Inspector Clouseau after you break wind during an interview or place your hand on your prospective employer's knee by mistake. These things happen. Don't kick yourself. Prepare for your next role.

What's the key to finding a job?

The key to finding a job is to try all the keys until you find the one that opens the door. If you know the correct key, make a duplicate. If you lose that key, it only costs a buck for another one.

What's the best part about looking for a job?

The best part is when you've got so many things happening, so many possibilities to consider, so many offices to imagine working in, that you find yourself saying, "First come, first served. Here I am. Come and get me," and other nonsense like that.

What are the bad parts?

There are no bad parts, only bad attitudes.

What should I say to people who want to know what I do for a living?

Some people say the worst part about being unemployed is telling people that you're unemployed. But think about it. You have an advantage. Those who have jobs can give only one answer. You can choose from a dozen or more, a veritable banquet of responses, depending on your mood.

Feeling coy? Flirtatious? Respond with, "What I do for work is not found in the Dictionary of Occupational Titles."

Pretending you heard wrong is a good defensive tool. "How's my slob-hunting? It's going quite well. I've found an excellent supply of both short- and long-term slobs to meet my needs." Or, "Yes, hog-jumping is a difficult skill to master. I'm shooting for the Olympics."

"This is a helluva way to find out what color my parachute is!"

Chapter Two
The History of Job-hunting

Where did job-hunting begin? Who was the first job-hunter? Who came first, the job-hunter or the job? These and other nagging questions keep many job-seekers awake at night. Unfortunately, the historical evidence of job-hunting is scanty and is limited to shards of the slab rock resumé of a Neanderthal man specializing in interior cave design and hieroglyphics for a support group of laid-off Egyptian pyramid builders.

Undaunted, we put our imaginations to work. Refusing to be yoked to loathsome factual research, we put together a Disneyland-style jungle cruise through the wild world of job-hunting. All aboard!

The first stop on our cruise is a visit to the world's most successful job-hunter. Say hello to Seymour Ardnocks and his dog, Headhunter, whom he calls "a job-hunter's best friend."

Us: How's the job-hunting going, Seymour?
Seymour: Couldn't be better. Going on my eighty-fifth year. Once job-huntin' gets in your blood, it won't let go.
Us: Ever find a job?
Seymour: Thousands. I'm good at what I do.
Us: Ever go to work for somebody?
Seymour: For a day or so. But I always seem to get fired about the second day on the job.
Us: Why?

Seymour: I'm a firm believer that the best time to look for a job is when you got one. First day on the job, I'll be making phone calls, sending out resumés. My employers don't like it. Sooner or later I'm out on the street.

Us: How have you supported yourself all these years?

Seymour: If you do what you love, the money will follow. I'm doing what I love. Money will follow, someday, I suppose.

Us: How did you get into the field?

Seymour: I knew early on what I wanted to be. My kindergarten classmates wanted to be nurses and airplane pilots. I always wanted to be a job-hunter. Looking for work—that's my vocation. I've had over 20,000 interviews. Proud of every one of them. I think I've got another 1,000 in me before the big employer in the sky calls me in for an interview.

Us: What do you like so much about job-hunting?

Seymour: The sport. I'm like the fisherman who bags a twenty-pound salmon and throws it back. Once I've got the job, the thrill is gone. I'm in it for the hunt. Take the time I bagged a job as vice-president of a major company.

Us: What happened?

Seymour: Told him "Thanks, but I'll keep looking." Still am. Now tell me about your business. That's a field I'm interested in. I'd like to set up an informational interview. Here's my resumé. . . .

At this point we understood why Headhunter was a job seeker's best friend. By this time his jaw was clamped firmly around our leg. Several hours later, nearly questioned to death, we escaped.

History tells us that the first job-hunters were a nomadic tribe who summered in the south of France sometime before the first Cannes Film Festival. One night the tribe was sitting around the campfire belting out a few songs and planning the next day's activities: hiking, hunting, going to the beach, or hanging out. In a moment of rare candor, a tribe member confessed he was "burned-out on hunting."

A motion to hunt for a job was suggested, seconded, and carried with little debate, as it was late and they were ready to roll into their tents. Most probably thought that looking for work might be a fun game, like hide-and-seek. Boy, were they wrong.

The next day the tribe members got up extra early and fanned out into the woods to seek work. Although only one person was successful—he snagged a part-time job as a tour guide—others reported a couple of good leads. Some even lined up interviews. The tribe continued to job-hunt and discovered that they had a certain flair for it. They quickly developed networking skills during their forays into the woods, maintained frequent contact with every person or animal they encountered, and fine-tuned their interviewing skills.

Soon every member in the tribe had lined up a full-time job with benefits, perks, and an office with a window. Clearly, the tribe had the right kind of noses for sniffing out employers. Many of them later became successful head-hunters themselves. The descendants of these successful job-hunters found their niche in the junk bonds industry just a few short centuries later.

Job-hunting hit a difficult, unproductive period during the Dark Ages. This was a dismal time because people did their looking during the night after everyone had gone home. The few who were successful found jobs on the graveyard shift. By contrast, job-hunting came into its own during the Renaissance. Looking for work evolved into a fine art, as well as a college elective. Adult education centers included it in their catalogs. Job-hunters were revered— even idolized— for their skills.

Rush hours were enlivened by job-seeking minstrels singing ballads of achievement. Cover letters took form in four-act plays and operas. On the down side, valuable job-hunting time was lost because a good resumé was considered incomplete if it contained less than 100 handwritten pages. The extreme length, combined with typos, meant that job-hunters spent more time writing their resumés than looking for work.

But who wanted to look for work when the Renaissance was going on right outside your door? When your buddy dropped by and said, "Hey, let's go to the Renaissance," you went, knowing that the Renaissance didn't roll around every four years like the Olympics. Besides, admission was free, and who could concentrate on writing a resumé with all the commotion and the smell of piping hot pizza wafting from the Renaissance?

The next stop on our cruise ("Watch out for those crocodiles—they haven't had a job-hunter in months") is a visit to Herb, proprietor of Herb's Temp-for-Tips employment agency. Herb's been in the business since he dropped out of junior high school and prides himself as something of a "job-hunting history buff." A talk with him always brings perspective to the historical.

Herb leaned back, added some kerosene to the fire, and warmed up some soft drinks. This is what he told us:

> For my money, the best job-hunters were the Spaniards around 1500. Or was it 1800? Anyway, they were called explorers, but actually they were job-hunters who traveled great distances to make 'cold calls' on unknown lands. Most people don't know that.

We didn't, either.

Take that feller Columbus. Although he wasn't a Spaniard, Columbus rightly believed his job-hunting prospects would be improved if he had Spain's King Ferdinand and Queen Isabella as references. He had the right idea, but despite several interviews, we all know that Columbus never got a job in the New World. Naturally, he was disappointed, having voyaged thousands of miles across the Atlantic Ocean. But, really, he could only blame himself for forgetting his resumé. Sure, he was given the title Discoverer of the New World, but the job didn't pay, and Columbus died poor and without retirement benefits.

Other job-hunters followed Columbus. Some started as interns in the New World to get their foot in the door. The experience paid off, and many found full-time jobs as outlaws and brothel owners.

Herb also filled us in on the Vikings, who are purported to be the first job-hunters/explorers in the New World.

Fact is, they were unsuccessful because nobody wanted to hire people with horns sticking out of their helmets; their headgear could be dangerous, especially in narrow hallways. The Vikings never understood how to dress for an interview. They went back to Norway and resumed their search for work in the fjords.

The first job-hunters in America were the Pilgrims, who many believe came to escape religious persecution. Actually, they were escaping tyrannical bosses in England. They wanted to become their own tyrannical bosses. They settled for work as Puritans, which really wasn't that much different. Although their first year was hard, the Pilgrims and Native American hosts got together for a potluck in late November to talk turkey and network—a custom that persists today.

Lewis and Clark led a famous job expedition. The boys came back empty-handed, but with a lot of good leads. Lewis and Clark later founded a career-counseling/fur-trapping business so the expedition wasn't a complete failure.

Let's change gears and get sentimental and teary-eyed. We'll stop by to see Grandpappy Johnson, for his happy, if foggy, memories of his job-hunting days and the comfort of days gone by.

Grandpappy told us of a boyhood spent on the job-hunting trail, a narrow, two-lane path with several dead-man's curves. "We'd meet up with other job-hunters and sing songs as we walked the twenty-five miles or more each day to call on a country store or blacksmith. We didn't have any fancy resumés, cover letters, or employment agencies like you folks have today. You job-hunters have it so easy." We cut Grandpappy Johnson off here as the "good old days" were getting boring. Back to our history lesson.

America has had its share of noteworthy job-hunters, the would-be employed who stood up, risking their lives for work. Revolutionary War hero Nathan Hale said, "Give me a job, or give me death." Well, he didn't get the job, but he paved the way for many in this country to find work. We remember them now:

"I have only begun to look for a job," responded John Paul Jones to the British request to halt his job search.

"I shall return," General Douglas MacArthur said, after he was turned down as a sushi chef in Japan.

"Why don't you come up and see me sometime?" was Mae West's brave attempt to get a job.

Consider the heroism of the Civil War's Admiral David Farragut, who said, "Damn the torpedoes. There's a full-time job ahead."

We can also learn from the mistakes of some pretty famous people. "I'm no crook," answered Richard Nixon to an interviewer questioning his honesty. Now here was a guy who knew how to stress the positive. Nixon never got another job.

We would be remiss if we didn't mention the contributions of women. Although they got a late start, women have been great job-hunters from the git-go when a woman announced, "If I don't get out of this &*!#@ house, I'll go stir-crazy!"

Joan of Arc was one great female job-hunter who skipped middle management altogether on her way to the top. Joan applied for and got a high-powered, if temporary, job as a saint after she accepted an offer from the Big Employer to lead the French to greatness. Regrettably, she was later burned at the stake.

Margaret Thatcher used a stiff upper lip and an immovable coiffure to get a job as Prime Minister of Great Britain. She ruled with an iron fist—and an iron hairdo—for many years. One of her great accomplishments was her defeat of Argentina, which surrendered when she threatened to impose the same hairstyle on all Argentinians unless they gave up the Falklands.

At our final stop, we have the privilege of viewing excerpts from a job-hunter's journal. These entries were found in the glove compartment of a '57 Studebaker by an enterprising junkyard owner. He gave us the notes in exchange for our hubcaps.

Day one in the unemployment line

Clem, who processes the claims, has become quite the entrepreneur. "What can I do for you today?" he asked as I crawled to his window after waiting in line for an hour. He offered a hot towel, handed me a warmed-over job lead, and poured me a glass of bottled water. I dropped an extra fifty cents into his tip cup after I got my check.

I have a great desire to be of use, to be needed. So, on my way home, I saw a teenager squeezing a pimple. I asked if he could use somebody on a part-time basis through the challenging adolescent years.

Day two

Flo, my career counselor, called. She suggested that I think about a career outside the public and private sectors.

I rewarded myself for a good day with a bottle of Cabernet to go with my Big Mac and large fries. Lined up fourteen informational interviews, one with the garbage collector who says you learn a lot about life from what people throw away. I will ride around with him one morning. Lined up another with the paper boy, who tells me that information is power.

Perhaps job-hunting is just not in my blood. I abhor the hunt, the kill. Rather, I'm a gatherer. I amass, cull, glean. Make note to invite hiring managers over for borscht.

Day three

When you lose your job, you're a nobody. My mother hasn't returned my calls. My kid sister says she's been in a meeting with my teenage brother.

What is job-hunting anyway? Is it an art? If so, where's the model? If it's a science, am I missing the lab? Did I make a fatal mistake when I said I liked the job, but I had reservations about the work setting? It's in the middle of a cornfield. Gnats, my prospective employer said, would be a drawback I'd have to learn to live with. I noticed the employees offhandedly waving at clouds of gnats and swatting themselves while working at their typewriters. Productivity could be better, he admitted.

Day four

Saw my former boss today as I was passing by a lunchtime Nazi Party rally. I realize now that we had different styles. I recall that afternoons were the times he liked to crack the whip. Nevertheless, I worked the crowd for job leads.

I ponder the big questions: How can I get to the hiring manager? Can I get back in with a hand stamp?

Day five

Today I had an interview at a place where the receptionist is more interesting than the job. Took a test at an agency that supplies temps for manicurist shops. Did twenty-three nails in three minutes, which I thought was pretty good, but they told me to work on my speed and come back.

Siphoned gas from a Mercede-Benz. I left a note explaining my situation and said I would pay it back when (1) I got a job or (2) I switched to a handmower.

Sent out thank-you notes. Still, it depresses me that nobody writes or calls to say, "You're welcome."

Day six

Job-hunting has become obsessive. Taking a

walk last night, I came upon a young couple necking in the park. I asked if they needed any help.

I met Flo for coffee this morning. She suggested I return to school. No way! I'm not repeating seventh grade. Asking a girl to the sock hop was enough trauma for one lifetime.

Day seven

Last night I dreamed I got hired. The only stipulation was that I had to work horizontally. I negotiated a 90-degree angle.

I still think the job-hunting blues would sound better if played on the banjo.

Day eight

"No job's perfect," Flo told me after an interview. The position pays well, and there's an opportunity for growth, but my office is in the men's bathroom.

I find myself fantasizing about owning my own business. Perhaps starting up the Foreign Legion somewhere near Carlsbad Caverns, or opening up a bed-and-breakfast within a camel's ride of the Pyramids.

Day nine

Today I found work! Took a twenty-hour-per-week job as a donor to a sperm bank. I'm in population sales, I tell friends.

Clearly, our ramble through the history of job-hunting has given us clues as to its promising future, but questions remain. Will we do it on moving sidewalks? Will a job-hunting gene be found? If life can be created from sperm and egg, can a job be artificially produced through the union of hiring manager and job-seeker? Who will be the first job-hunter on Mars? If job-hunters formed their own country, would getting hired mean expulsion? Will the resumé go the way of the Edsel?

And what about job-hunting in the hereafter? Are job counselors provided? Is the work search down there living hell, an endless process of interviews and rejection letters? Is heaven a cushy desk job with plenty of sharpened No. 2 pencils?

It's an exciting future, one you won't want to miss.

"If you said it once, you've said it a thousand times. The hardest part of looking for a job is dragging around your resumé."

Chapter Three
Job-hunting around the World

People in other countries look for jobs in ways that may seem crazy to us. Each culture has its unique set of values, its quirks that go with looking for a job. What gets your foot in the door in Pakistan gets it cut off in Syria. And vice versa. Some of the techniques for job-hunting may seem a bit odd, others slightly kinky. Why should we care how the people of Istanbul seek snake-charming work, or why Moldavians bring their pets to interviews?

Answer: Global economy.

You've heard about it, seen commercials for it on TV. The best way to describe it is to say that the world's economy will soon be connected like you and the long-lost cousins in eastern Iran you've heard about but will never see.

Everything will be interrelated, a sort of "We Are the World" of business. What this means is that when a yak shepherd in southern Tibet sells his product, you will be affected because the price of yak meat will go up at your corner grocery store. Or soon you'll be trading your Barry Bonds baseball card for someone named Yomuni Masanki.

The more you know about the customs of the world, the better your job-hunting chances will be in the new global economy. To get you started thinking beyond the borders of the United States, here are a few important facts about the economy of other countries.

▲ In Sweden, The Institute for Smorgasbord Research employs 60 percent of all smorgasbord workers worldwide.

▲ In Madagascar, expertise with the Hula-Hoop is considered a symbol of fertility if twirled clockwise, joblessness if rotated counterclockwise.

▲ Small talk in Saudi Arabia focuses on camel humps, whereas in Australia it begins with clichés about the health of your lawn.

▲ In Japan, the varying weight of sumo wrestlers is the accepted way to start a business conversation ("Boy, Sako has gotten into the chocolate chip cookies . . . big-time.")

Be aware of differences.

People from former Soviet states are just now starting to formulate their own diverse rules for securing a job. Mistakes are being made. We are told of the job-hunter who brought a bottle of vodka to his job interview. His mistake: he didn't bring two glasses.

Some people are learning to transfer their skills to find new work. Laid-off KGB agents are securing employment in used car sales and aluminum siding, using their skills in intimidation to make big bucks. They are now freer to be their own bosses, and a few have become successful entrepreneurs.

A popular custom is the practice of standing in line while waiting for food, toilet paper, and other necessities. Former USSR citizens are now using this activity to network, as the following example shows:

> **Networksker:** We got a free market, but we're still standing in line, eh Comrade . . . er, I mean, buddy. What have the recent changes meant for

you? You still working at the Ministry of Propaganda?

Networkski: No, but I'm still working in propaganda. I'm now in advertising and PR. We're looking for good writers. Do you have experience writing in the lawnchair business?

In Japan, where workers are employed by the same company for life, only one job search per lifetime is allowed. It is taken very seriously. That is why the final interview is held at a karaoke lounge. The job-hunter must sing several Barbra Streisand or Neil Diamond songs while eating sushi. Then, packed into a bullet train with several corporate operatives, the job-hunter is mercilessly grilled. It is an odd custom, but one that has worked well for the Japanese, whose economy is considered second to none.

Consider the four rules of job-hunting as practiced in China:

1. Never wear Bermuda shorts to a first interview.
2. Know this Chinese proverb: "Smelly feet are an employer's best friend—if he likes smelly employees."
3. Bring at least ten family references to an interview.
4. Never use that Confucius cliché: "Maybe I *should* see a headshrinker, but I still say it's a crazy world out there."

Norwegians are a hardworking lot whose lust for life and pickled herring is legendary. Note that Norwegians are born skiing, and consider it a form of natural childbirth. Not surprisingly, interviews frequently take place while schussing down mountainsides, traversing the tundra on cross-country skis, or doing figure eights on ice.

Joblessness is next to cleanliness in Sweden, where job-hunters and company executives sweat out the final interview in a sauna. Swedes believe, "Open pores mean good employees."

Our friends the Brits used to own half the world, but today they languish as equal allies. Still, the British love to talk about the good old days. Interviews usually begin there with small talk about the Battle of Waterloo (they usually skip the American Revolution) and end with a few words about the Battle of Britain.

If jobs in your field of expertise are scarce, consider global job-hunting. Whereas you were once more or less confined to pounding the pavement in the United States, you may now investigate cottage industries in Mongolia, Iceland, Poland, and the southern portion of the Amazon.

When you expand your territory to the entire world, you'll never run out of cold calls. Given the different time zones, you can cold call any time of day. Remember, when it's 4 a.m. in Iowa, it's the start of the business day in Bangkok.

Subscribe to at least one newspaper per country, and two in Belgium, where French and Flemish are spoken. Hire a translator to go over the Want Ads in the business section. Your job-hunting will take on an international dimension when you come across companies with names like Kat Gut Tongue, Inc., which is currently seeking someone with your experience.

Sometimes the shotgun approach works. Target an entire country—Peru, for example—and send your resumé to every company listed. Tuesday do Brazil, and so forth, until you've covered the entire globe. By the time you've finished, you'll have established a worldwide reputation for thoroughness and possibly have some interviews set up.

Let's look at a few countries and consider strategies for gaining access to key hiring managers through international phone calls.

♠ **Japan**   Impress your listener by performing a Japanese tea ceremony over the phone. Or open the conversation by singing along with your karaoke machine. Longtime favorites sure to win you points are "Feelings" and "I Got You, Babe."

The Japanese are big sports fans. A little white lie that you are founder and president of your town's local sumo wrestling chapter is sure to win you points.

The Japanese are also big baseball fans. Keep up with the standings on the big island. Start a discourse over who was better—Sadaharu Oh or Babe Ruth—then segue into your own achievements.

♠ **Germany**   The Wall. You knocked one down between your living room and kitchen; they knocked one down between East and West. You've got something in common.

♠ **China**   Sure, this country is a long way from capitalism, but it's never too soon to make contacts. Establish your commonality by talking about your food-poisoning adventure on your last visit to Chinatown. Mention chop suey. Recite some Confucius or make up your own: "Confucius say he who looks for job in land of chow mein is three meals ahead of the game." Impress them with the fact that you had a Fu Manchu mustache during your adolescence. Say you'll call back in a few years to see if the government has changed.

♠ **France**   There is only one way for an American to get a job with a French company: Jerry Lewis. The French have anointed him a cultural icon. Rent several Lewis classics like *The Nutty Professor* or *The Bell Boy,* and study them so you have something interesting to talk about during your interview. Devise your own Jerry Lewis self-testing quiz. Try

Jerry's "terrible twos" trademark wail over the phone to a Renault executive.

▲ **Sweden** Land of smorgasbord. "I can eat smorgasbord every day," will get the ball rolling.

As you can see, job-hunting is no longer a local affair. As you become a globe-trotting job-seeker, you'll have the added pleasure of experiencing the world while you look for work. Remember, it's a global economy, and the whole world is hiring.

"Here's the way it works. I get you a job. You give me
your soul."

Chapter Four
The Job Search

Looking for a job means activating the brain's job-seeking impulses. These are sets of reflexes that lie dormant during periods of normal employment. However, phrases like "You're fired," "We're taking you off sales and putting you on unemployment," or "The boat is leaving and you're not on it" activate certain job-hunting hormones in the body.

But before you can become a successful job-hunter, you must go through several psychological stages associated with traumatic events.

1. **Shock and Denial** In the initial stage, the would-be job-hunter responds to "You need to clean out your desk" with "But I just vacuumed it last week." Sudden loss of control of the sphincter muscle has also been reported.

2. **Fear and Anxiety** Cold sweats and earwax buildup are typical physical responses to the cutoff of office supplies, copy machine privileges, and long-distance phone calls, to say nothing of the ready cash to buy underwear.

3. **Anger and Blame** In this stage, the victim seeks a scapegoat. Convenient targets are the boss who interrupted afternoon naps, a secretary who couldn't break the 200-words-per-minute typing barrier, slow elevators, Nixon, the Warsaw Pact.

4. **Self-blame, Shame, and Guilt** This phase is characterized by attempts to inflict harm on oneself. Predictable sadomasochistic behavior includes self-whipping with wet toilet paper and eating suppers of cornflake sandwiches.
5. **Despair and Depression** The would-be pavement-pounder hits bottom, unable to gather the strength to clip unsightly nose hairs or remove last week's mascara.
6. **Acceptance** Now, ready to hit the streets, the unemployed person takes on the new identity of job-hunting person.

On call twenty-four hours a day, the job search now becomes the breath of life, the one thing to live for. The job-hunting person gorges on leads, and over-indulges on late night cold calls. Job-hunting people see themselves as commander-in-chiefs of their personal "Invasion of the Job-Hunter." Job-hunting consumes them, and they consume it, along with extra helpings of fried clams. The result is a full-scale, amphibious assault on hiring managers. Job-hunters begin the search by assembling certain tools of the trade, a sort of toilet kit for the unemployed. Some of these items are:

The Resumé

No matter how creative your resumé is, it's not going to do you any good unless you can get it to the top of the compost heap. Here is a bushel of creative ways to give your resumé visibility.

▲ **Tattoo your resumé on your hinie** No more will you say, "Gee, I don't have my resumé with me," to a potential hiring manager. Tattooed resumés are the perfect antidote for companies trying to get rid of you by asking you to send your resumé. Here's a way to flash your resumé and gain an interview at the same time. Tattooed resumés are usually short (the hobby section is almost always omitted). Note: This method is not for those with low pain thresholds.

▲ **Bathroom resumés** Remember bathroom-users tend to be hiring managers, and vice versa. Produce resumé stickers, then attach them to bathroom stalls with clever headlines like, "I'm glad you got a chance to sit down and look at my resumé," or "Don't flush this opportunity down the toilet."

▲ **Flyer resumés** Beat the crowd to the sports stadium and place a copy of your resumé on every seat. Hawk peanuts and your skills to 50,000 resumé-hungry fans.

▲ **Subliminal advertising** After you've had a promising interview, leave behind a remote-controlled tape recorder with the repeating message: "(Your name) is the best candidate for the job." This will help you leap over more qualified candidates. (It's rumored that Richard Nixon used this strategy to secure the vice-presidential nomination as running mate to Dwight Eisenhower.)

Networking

Another vital part of your kit is networking. To job-hunters, every encounter with another member of the human species, or with an extra-smart chimpanzee, is reason to yak, schmooze, or network.

Networking is something you can do on a bus, in a line at the post office, in a public restroom—wherever and whenever.

Small Talk

One of the important elements of networking is small talk, invented by an association of insurance salesmen. Small talk is defined as conversation that is erased from short-term memory as it is being spoken. It is the language of business.

Small talk should last no more than two minutes and should end when somebody says, "You're boring me to death with all this small talk. What's really on your mind?"

The objective of small talk is to begin the conversation by talking about anything but business and to find some common ground.

Example 1

Networker: Bill tells me you're a practicing vampire. What a great hobby! He says you like to drink your own blood and that you occasionally get together with a group of friends and sample each other's hearty red.

Networkee: Darn right. In fact, Bill's one of the gang and, I might add, a guy with a great banquet.

Networker: I'm new to the sport, but I'd love to join you for a drink—and to talk about current developments in the industry.

Networkee: How about Thursday? We'll get a chance to see what you're made of.

Networker: Sure. I'll bring the cheese and crackers.

Example 2

Networker: Sally said to say hello to you. While I was at Human Resources, she and I had a sordid, ill-conceived affair that coincidentally ended along with my job.

Networkee: Gee, I haven't seen Sally in about a

month. Actually, since I got the clap from her.
Networker: Well, what do you know? We've got something in common after all.
Networkee: Whadayaknow!

An excellent way to network is to join an association of your peers. At after-work events, you can enjoy the company of others while you network. Ask one of your peers about a particular company you are investigating.

Example

> **Networker:** Thanks John. Before I leave this wonderful party and find some real food, I wonder if you might share your opinion about what is happening in the marketing department before I give a call.
> **Peer:** Fire away.
> **Networker:** What seem to be some of the department's key challenges?
> **Peer:** Well, for one, we've been steadily losing market share in our line of frozen cat food. I think it may have something to do with quality. Sales have fallen off since we replaced the tuna extract with bits of dried bathtub scum.
> **Networker:** I see. Has any consumer testing been done on the new products?
> **Peer:** Yes, but only on humans, who liked it just fine. By the way, did you try the paté?

Be forewarned, networking takes guts. There are folks out there you would rather not talk to. Yet these people may have job leads with names and phone numbers. You can't afford to ignore them. What? You'd rather attend a nail biting contest than grovel for information? Bite your nails to the quick, then start networking in person or via Alexander Graham Bell.

For example, the sleaze bag who slept with your wife is also a hiring manager. What do you do? Turn the situation to your advantage. Praise him for his good taste, then press for job leads.

Or, you've heard that the guy who broke your nose twenty-five years ago might help. Compliment him on his right jab, then counterpunch with a request for quick hits on who's hiring.

Remember to delegate networking responsibilities. Involve every member of your family, from your kids to your third cousin twice removed. Stay on their tails.

Now, let's get your kids in the act. Remember that they have access to hundreds of contacts through school. A job may be only as far away as another parent.

Send your kids to school with express instructions to find out what their classmates' parents do. Give each child a quota of five kids (five parents) per day. Failure means immediate grounding and forced vegetable feedings. If any lead looks promising, order your child to invite the prospective job lead over for drinks after the school play. Be sure to meet the parents. Shake hands, then plunge in. "My Jimmy tells me you're in the hot tub business. I've got experience in that area. . . ." and you're on your way.

Put your mother to work for you. It's the newest job-hunting technique. She's the only person who can add that extra ingredient to get you a job: guilt. She's also a great reference. Mothers will lay down their lives for their kids, so you know they'll do what it takes to help you find a job.

Get your mother on the phone. Have her badger companies you haven't been able to crack. She'll know what to do and be glad to help you get back to work.

Here's an actual transcript of a taped conversation from the phone of a job-hunter's mother.

Manager: Hello, this is Mr. Frankfurter.

Mother: You should be ashamed of yourself.

Manager: Whah?

Mother: My son, Harold, called you three times. You didn't return his phone calls. Didn't your mother teach you any manners?

Manager: Well, yes, she did but . . .

Mother: Yes, what?

Manager: Yes, ma'am.

Mother: That's better. My son is also on the phone—say hello Harold.

Son: Hello, Mr. Frankfurter.

Mother: My son is a good boy. He has good work habits. What else do you need to know? He took out the trash when I told him to. He kept his room neat—okay, he didn't always make his bed—but he's a good boy. I'm his reference. I raised him. I know how he runs. He's a hard worker.

Manager: He just seems a little shy on experience for the job. One year of bagging groceries does not qualify him to be our advertising manager.

Mother: Listen, Mr. Big Shot! He'll learn on the job. You learned on the job, didn't you?.

Manager: Well, sure I . . .

Mother: Of course you did! What's the point of starting a job you already know how to do? Did I know how to raise Harold before I had him? No, but I did it anyway, and I did a pretty good job.

Manager: I see . . .

Mother: Do you eat?

Manager: Of course.

Mother: You sound hungry. We'll bring some soup over—my son and I—and we'll talk about the job. Just the three of us. You'll feel better. You don't sound so good.

Manager: We'll just talk?
Mother: We'll be there in five seconds.
Manager: Five seconds?
Mother: Yes, we're calling from the lobby.

Don't be afraid to ask Mom to help you out. You may feel a little wormy in the act, but if it gets you a job, who cares?

Religious networking

In the spirit of religious freedom, embrace every religion. You should be hitting two or three synagogues on any given Saturday. Sunday, too, is no longer a day of rest; it's a day of Mass. Take Communion several times. Donate your services to those in any congregation by leaving your "For Hire" business card when the hat is passed. Meditate with the Buddhists. If you pray at enough places, someone's bound to hear you.

Synagogues and Chinese gambling dens are good places to enlarge your vocabulary as well as to make connections.

During your visits to synagogues, use the catch-all Yiddish expression, "Oye vay," with every opportunity. As in, "Oye vay, do you know where the bathrooms are?" or "Oye vay, the Cubs look good this year." If that's not working, try, "Oye gevalt," as in "Oye gevalt, what do you do for a living?"

Catechism and *Pope* are popular terms among Catholics. When it's Sunday-go-to-meetin' time, try, as conversation openers, "They don't do catechism like they used to," or "Who's your favorite Pope of all time?"

Political networking

When it comes to politics, you have to be a Democrat, a Republican, and a reformed Communist. People who vote have jobs. Attend their meetings. Play the game of politics. Promise to deliver your neighborhood to the local politico. Increase your chances for a job by making this offer to both major political parties. Either way, one of your candidates wins and you win. Then demand a job. Tit for tat.

Transportation networking

Transportation centers are filled with busy businesspeople whom you need only coax, scold, or occasionally whip to provide assistance. Plant yourself at the airline terminal gate. When people start pouring from the plane, hand them your resumé while shouting, "Business information that could change your life!" Offer to drive well-dressed businesspeople to their appointments. Don't let them out of your car until they've passed on several nuggets of job-related information.

Consider taking a short commuter flight to ensure a captive audience. After the plane has taken off, simply go up and down the aisles making contacts. You'll be able to meet hundreds of fully employed people on a round-trip basis. If your cash flow is low, stow away.

Public transportation offers great networking possibilities. The subway, particularly when it breaks down, is an excellent place to network. Turn the situation to your advantage. A crowded bus is reason to rejoice, not complain. You've got a captive audience. Use the opportunity. Ask strap-hangers if they're going to be late for work. Be prepared with follow-up questions. What kind of work? Is there any work available?

Networking resources

Although networking is considered the best way to find a job, your job-hunting kit should include several books to guide you through the process. Dozens of books have been devoted to the hullabaloo of job-hunting. Some of the newer books have additional uses. *Hitting the Beaches: Job-Hunting Tips for Guam* is a good bedtime read sure to put you to sleep. Madonna's *Hot and Sultry Job Tips* is suitable bathroom reading.

Our inside sources in the publishing industry tipped us off on these new releases that offer a fresh perspective:

Interviews That Get Nose Jobs This is a complete guide to where the nose jobs are, the hidden nose job market, how to find your nose job in a nostril-impaired economy, and how to sniff out a job. Michael Jackson has made millions since he had his nose refigured, while Jimmy Durante—with his original, unstreamlined shnoz—is dead and presumed to be unemployed.

Hot Jobs for the Next Century Although this book was written in 1869, remember that the job market tends to come full circle. Consider night classes for a career in blacksmithing or repairing hoop skirts.

Landing a Job in 60 Seconds or Less This is a pamphlet packed with information on blackmail etiquette or, if you prefer, on how to double your chances for a second interview through the use of a simple death threat.

Jobs in the Black Market The Black Market, once scorned by job-hunters for its lack of benefits, flex-time hours, and on-site laundry, may be worth a second look.

Calling for Work: Twenty Animal Calls to Attract Hiring Managers Develop your animal magnetism with inventive "job-howling" techniques. Have employers knocking at your door with mating calls imported from Antarctica—a land with virtually no unemployment. Also includes sections on "Barking up the Right Tree," "Primal Yelps," "Chirping for Part-time Work," and "When to Use Hyena Laughs During Interviews. "

The Interview: What to Wear

It's time for the Big Interview. Wondering what to wear? Think about standing out from the crowd while fitting in. Sound contradictory? It's not. Here are some suggestions.

Cross-dressing Are you a man interviewing in an office dominated by women? Increase your chances by wearing clothes of the opposite gender. The look says: "I'm a man, but I've got a feminine side," and vice-versa.

To men: Don't forget to shave your legs, and nothing bigger than a 34B cup. See the movie *Tootsie* at least twice. Practice putting on your makeup a few times before you hit the trail.

To women: Show you can be one of the guys by attaching a "medium" jock strap to your briefcase and wearing a baseball cap backwards.

Androgynous dressing The gender issue becomes moot with this look that says: "Here I am. What am I? "
    Taking hormone shots is a hot job-hunting technique sure to separate you from the pack. For women, your interview preparation includes a healthy shot of testosterone to deepen your voice and increase facial hair that you can shape into a goatee or muttonchops for just the right hint of masculinity. Men's options include an injection that develops the bustline and pitches the voice in the soprano range. Be sure to confuse your interviewer by sprinkling your conversation with phrases like, "It's that time of the month—when I give the car a tune-up," or "On Sundays I just like to watch football—while I knit."

Combo dressing Flexibility is what employers want these days, and the miniskirt-with-wing-tips ensemble is sure to put points on your scoreboard. It's skimpy, yet cloddy, and it's a great way to save on shoes. Your message is clear: "I'm sexy, but my feet are planted firmly on the ground."

Rent a Stand-in

Some of us just can't get the hang of being interviewed. That's okay. Hire a charm school graduate, or a seasonal sales rep to stand in for you. These specialists make a great first impression. Of course, you can expect a few raised eyebrows when you show up for the first day of work.

The Interview: What to Know

At some point, you will be called for an interview. Here are the correct answers to some commonly asked questions.

1. How do you get the interview off to a good start?
Most people think the first thing to do is shake hands. Wrong. Hand over the remains from last night's supper, a cigar, or a breath mint. Employers are looking for people who can help them, generous employees. Make them think you'll be the kind of employee who'll be offering free show tickets every other day. You can reverse the course—after you've been hired—by asking your boss for freebies.

2. How do you project an assertive personality?
Take control of the interview by grabbing the seat normally reserved for your interviewer. Pepper your prospective employer with questions about experience and qualifications. After a few minutes, say, "I just wanted to show you I'm a person who can take charge of the situation. Now it's your turn." You'll have established your unique style.

3. How do you prove you can come up with creative solutions to problems?

Break into song at various points during the interview. A couple of suggestions are verses from "We Can Work It Out" (the Beatles) or "I Did It My Way" (Frank Sinatra). If the interviewer joins in on the chorus, you're on your way.

4. What is the best way to answer the question, "What are your weaknesses?"

This is an annoying question that interviewers get from reading books on how to interview. Don't fall into the trap. A sarcastic retort works best. Answer, "Weak ankles. I don't skate well," or "I have a weakness for hot fudge sundaes, but it has yet to interfere with my work."

5. Is playing hard-to-get a good strategy?

You want to convey that you are in demand. Buy a beeper and set it to go off every five minutes. Tell the interviewer it's another company requesting an interview.

6. What do you say when are asked how you got along with your former boss and co-workers?

Convince your prospective employer that you work well with people. Your stock answer is: "I see my past corporate experience as similar to growing up in a dysfunctional family." This answer is sure to win you points because your interviewer will be thinking about his or her own family's wacked-out episodes. If your interviewer *doesn't* come from a dysfunctional family, you don't want to work there. The place is just too weird.

7. How do you answer the question, "Why did you leave your last job?"

This is a trick question you can easily evade by turning the negative into the positive. "I was a victim of my own success." Or, "I left with my honor, if not my job. People were relying on my expertise too much. I felt they would reach their potential only if I let them fend for themselves."

8. What do you say when the interviewer asks if you have any questions for him or her?

Here's your chance to shine: Probe the interviewer's personal hygiene habits. Who's on the make in the office? What size paper clips does the firm use? Stuff like that. This will separate you from the crowd.

9. What should you say when asked if there is anything else the company should know about you?

Here is the perfect opportunity to reassure your interviewer that, despite evidence to the contrary, your flatulence is under control. Assure your interviewer that you are seeing a specialist and that it hasn't been an issue at any of the other one-person offices you've worked at.

10. How should you end the interview?

Most people end the interview with a polite "thank you." That's not enough in today's competitive job market. Offer a racetrack tip or some good betting action. Hand your prospective boss a package of underwear you got on sale. Your interviewer will be impressed by your cost-saving skills.

"I'm not sure I can accept 'recovery from a dysfuntional company' as the reason for not having worked the last five years."

Chapter Five
The Twenty-four-hour-a-day Job Search

Remember the good old days when looking for work was just a full-time job?

Today's competitive market often requires a twenty-four-hour-a-day job search. At the minimum. Learn to eat, sleep, and play while you look for a job. You can always catch up on your shuteye when you're back at work.

Want proof that twenty-four-hour-a-day job-hunting really works? In laboratory tests, 90 percent of white mice got high-powered jobs 8.6 times faster using the round-the-clock approach. If it worked for unemployed mice, it can certainly work for you. Here's how.

Use Your Saturday Nights

Spend your Saturday nights cozying up with the classifieds. Forget about movies, parties, and friends, and start getting those letters and resumés out by fax and overnight express. Leave voice mail messages that say, "I'm sorry I was unable to reach you on Saturday night. . . ." Prospective employers will be very impressed when they hear that you took the time to leave a personal message for them.

Dress the Part

Don't be caught without your business suit on. Looking for work requires that you be in a job-search mode 'round the clock.

Fortunately, the fashion industry has recognized the trend for all-day job-hunting and developed a variety of styles that state "I'm W-2 material."

Ensuring you'll be thinking about the next day's job-hunting activities are your pinstriped slippers and power bathrobe emblazoned with the words, "I'm a Looking-for-Work-aholic."

On hot summer days, when thousands flock to the beaches, you'll be there too—networking. Dressed in your lightweight, quick-drying, corporate gray swimsuit and polka dot tie for men, or one-piece suit with bow-tie for women, you'll work the beach in comfort, passing out resumés, and slapping suntan oil on the backs of well-heeled beachgoers.

You'll be all business on the ski slopes in the warmth of your insulated pantyhose and black pump-style ski boots. Pass out your resumé on the lift line. Choose a prospect to ride up with, then harangue your captive seat mate with the details of your experience. Refuse to lift the safety bar until you've made several contacts. Make sure you accidentally crash into several expensively dressed skiers. Probe for information as you untangle yourself.

Stalk Your Prey

When you see a wild pack of job-hunters on the run waving resumés, you know they've just spotted a hiring manager. The hiring manager is the Holy Grail, the obscure object of desire: slippery, elusive, impossible to reach by phone, fax, or mail. You know you could get a job if you could just pin one down.

Ordinary means won't do—you must emulate the pros. Stalk hiring managers like the paparazzi—snapping their pictures as they leave their jobs at the end of the day. Make them feel like Jackie O. Learn from the masters of entrapment—bullfighters, collection agency employees, Rambo, snake charmers. Kidnapping a hiring manager is now considered a legitimate job-hunting technique.

Network Nonstop

Studies have shown that successful job-hunters contact at least 500,000 people. That may sound like a lot, but it's really only ten people per minute, seven days a week. Get networking; time's a-wasting!

If you dress for success, you can make contacts anywhere and everywhere. Introduce yourself and hand out resumés wherever you go.

Let's begin with an ordinary shopping trip. Work that supermarket or mall like a politician, shaking hands and kissing babies. Soon you'll be able to say, "I found my job over the broccoli."

Driving is a networking bonanza. Tailgate the movers and shakers who ride the highways every day. Spot a potential hiring manager in your rearview mirror while you're at the toll booth. Traffic can wait while you chat. Ask the toll-booth attendant to be on the lookout for you, too.

Work the Phones

Once you've made a list of everyone who fits into the category of "people aware of my existence since conception," you'll always have plenty of people to call.

Here's one example of a successful networking call to an "old friend."

> **Networker:** Is this the same Tom Smith who sat next to me in the first grade class at Smith Elementary?
> **Networkee:** Uh, yeah, I went to Smith. Who's this?
> **Networker:** It's Joe Jones. I've been thinking about you. What have you been doing?
> **Networkee:** Been doin' time, mostly.
> **Networker:** Oh, so you're not a hiring manager?
> **Networkee:** Well, depends. We got a bank job we could use a driver for.

A job lead! The networker in this example followed up with resumé and cover letter and emphasized his candy bar heist back in the fifth grade. Hey, a job's a job.

You can't just call people you know. Turn your cold calls into hot ones with sizzling small talk to randomly selected companies. Here's an example.

> **You:** I just called to tell you what a great job you've been doing. People just don't praise each other these days. My hat's off to you.
> **Networkee:** Who is this, anyway?
> **You:** Oh, one of your admirers.
> **Networkee:** Well, I like to think I've done a pretty good job.
> **You:** I'd love to hear more about it, down to the last detail. Shall we do lunch? Say, two o'clock, Wednesday?

Get Inside the Organization

Insider trading may be illegal; insider job-hunting is not. It's the only way to be sure that managers and human resource reps will see your resumé; it's a great way to prepare for interviews, and, most important of all, it is the ultimate way to uncover the hidden job market.

March into the HR department and create a diversion by announcing, "Hey, gang, I just spotted Kevin Costner in the cafeteria . . ." When everyone bolts, put your resumé on the manager's desk.

Act like one of the gang. Cruise the coffee stations and waltz by the water coolers, listening for gossip. Start conversations with, "So, what's this I hear about some new openings in the marketing department?" or "I hear Johnson is on her way out of here."

The hours after midnight are when you really get your job-hunting kicks in. Think of yourself as a crafty Sam Spade as you slip a trenchcoat over your janitor outfit and sneak into companies. They told you over the phone that they were looking over your resumé—now you can look them over. Rifle through hiring managers' desks and see what they're really up to. Look for possible blackmail opportunities—clues of an office affair or stashes of office supplies. Impress your interviewer with hot tips: "I shouldn't be telling you this, but . . ." Schedule yourself for appointments with all vice presidents. Add to your social schedule by noting upcoming company functions and show up with potato salad.

Here's your opportunity to see who your competition is—and get rid of it. It wasn't a good fit, anyway. Something better will come along.

When the sun comes up, chuck your overalls, and prepare for the new business day. Stick around. Establish squatter's rights. It'll be easier for them to hire you than to start eviction proceedings.

Follow Up: Operation Hire Me

With all this effort, you're sure to come up with some hot interviews. For these occasions, change from your everyday business suit into your knockout interview threads. Play it right and you can land the job with the first interview. Here's how:

▲ Communication is critical to a successful interview, so cut the hiring manager off from any unexpected disturbances; put a do-not-disturb sign on the door, snip the phone line, or give the secretary the day off.

▲ Master the latest B&B techniques—brainwashing and brown-nosing. Play a video of your accomplishments throughout the interview. Produce a subliminal audiotape with the message, "Hire me now." Put some muscle relaxant in your interviewer's coffee. Comment on your interviewer's work and interests, using the information you've gathered from your after-hours sleuthing.

▲ Show that you're a team player—bring your job-hunting team with you. They can include references—your fifth grade teacher, your former scout leader, your grandmother, a caterer with a ten-course lunch, a masseuse, and several high-powered consultants dispensing free business advice. Enliven the interview with a song-and-dance show, singing your praises.

▲ When the manager tries to end the interview, say politely but firmly that you've got all day—and so does your interviewer. Inform your interviewer that you've padlocked the door and cut the phone lines.

Market Yourself as a Product

Think of yourself as a product first, a person second. Sell yourself like a box of detergent, a vacuum cleaner, or an encyclopedia.

Bribery

Offer special incentives for your being hired—you'll give 150 percent for the first two months, a money-back guarantee, and you'll throw in a wash, cut, and blow dry—at no extra charge. Remember: when your boss looks good, you look good. Wear a bargain-basement price tag to show you are a great buy. And, of course, since you've been looking for a job twenty-four hours a day, you won't mind working twenty hours a day—the rest will do you good.

Advertising

Don't forget the power of advertising. Put a loudspeaker on your van and drive slowly through the financial district. Plaster your picture on billboards all over town. Hiring managers may not answer your calls, but they won't miss your mug as they drive by.

The sky's the limit, so put your name and qualifications everywhere. Resumés in bathroom stalls will give your captive audience something to read. Try a new spin on the old standby, "For a good time, call _____.References available upon request."

These days anybody can have his or her own cable TV show. If you don't prefer to sell yourself with your own paid-programming slot, make the rounds on the big-time talk shows with your story of being an unemployed spouse of a transsexual bigamist.

Follow the TV news crews. When the house lights come on, flash your phone number on a cue card.

Use Guerilla Tactics

Using these time-proven techniques will surely land your dream job in twenty-four hours—or a year at the very most. However, if by some chance things don't pan out, consider using some guerilla tactics that were successful in the Wild Job Kingdom.

▲ Plead guilty to somebody else's crime and take a year off in jail. Enjoy free room and board, employment in the prison library, and ever-changing networking possibilities.

▲ The fact is that the job market is not expanding. Therefore, you've got to create an opening. That means somebody has to leave.

▲ Consider a change of gender for a new start and better luck.

▲ Time for a career change? The future is in health care. Rework your resumé and *voila!* You're a brain surgeon.

▲ Relocate. You've got to go where the jobs are. Siberia and Iceland are hiring midlevel executives now! There are more hiring managers in Antarctica per capita than anywhere else in the world. Expand your horizons. Instead of targeting a company, set your sights on a continent.

▲ Retire. You may be only twenty-eight, but why not take pleasure in those golden years now while you're still young enough to enjoy them?

Looking for work is not just a job, it's a lifetime commitment. Once you've found a job, don't get complacent. Keep looking. Use the first day on the job to make some calls, set up several interviews, and send out your new resumés. Remember, job-hunting is the one job that nobody can take away from you.

"I think I'll take a day off from looking for a job."

Chapter Six

From the Back of the Unemployment Line

▼

Frequently, the search for a job takes on additional psychological dimensions because of your healthy obsession with finding work. You may experience occasional psychotic episodes in which you have an urge to lose your lunch on a human resources representative. This is quite normal and an important reason why human resources personnel wear raincoats indoors

Consider the experiences exhumed in the job-hunting log of Jerry Slingsdorf, an accountant seeking work in and around the Louisiana Bayou.

8:20 A.M.

I am at a job interview. Have been for twenty minutes. Waiting downstairs. My prospective employer is playing hard-to-get. The receptionist says, "Miss Buxton will be right with you. She is a very busy person. She knows you're here." Yes, I am here.

8:45 A.M.

I tell the receptionist that I'll wait outside Miss Buxton's office. What's the difference? I have an appointment. The only thing in the way is other people. People with papers and questions who are delaying our important meeting. The receptionist disagrees.

She doesn't understand. Doesn't see that Miss Buxton and I are meant to be together? Hopelessly intertwined in an emphatic business relationship. To work as a team. Side by side. Soon, we'll be initialing memos to each other. Holding countless passionate phone conversations. She'll say something like, "Jerry, can you see to it that the work on the Miller account is done by five? It's important."

And I'll say something like, "You bet," "Sure thing," or "No problema," if I'm feeling bilingual. After all, she liked (loved?) my resumé. She called me. I got a first interview with her. The dance of business begins to unfold. She probes the soul of my accounting experience. I feed her facts, historical nonfiction, and poetic license. In short, I lie. I grovel.

I practice safe interviewing, stopping short of going all the way, of spending our weekdays together for the next 2.3 years (according to a study by the Roper Institute). She clasps me to her executive breasts as a full-timer with salary, benefits, and an employee I.D. badge. Nine-to-five locked in a passionate embrace. Yes, I will promote, protect, and defend the company from competitors, hostile takeovers, or a precipitous drop in the Dow Jones. We are meant to be. Like Procter and Gamble. Sears and Roebuck. Harry and Leona Helmsley.

9:00 A.M.
The receptionist says Miss Buxton wants to see me—right after her nine o'clock. . . .Something's wrong. Miss Buxton's in trouble. As we sit here, there's a pot boiling over, a coup developing. They're trying to get rid of her. Miss Buxton. My

would-be boss, confidante, and guardian of yearly raises. I must get to her. She needs my help. My expertise. My cheerful good mornings, and commitment to giving 200 percent even during lunch. Well, at least for the first couple of weeks.

I must warn her. Help Miss Buxton escape from the meeting. I know a way out. A back door by the mailroom. We'll rendezvous.

I've come a long way. I've battled armies of cars on narrow ribbons of highways, been delayed by stop signs and red lights intent on preventing our meeting. The consummation. The W-2 forms. The polite introduction to co-workers. The company handbook of rules and regulations. Oh, it's going to be good, so good.

On behalf of all people throughout the job-seeking world, oh receptionist of neutrality, please, the letter of transit to see Miss Buxton.

9:30 A.M.
My strength is ebbing, my stomach growling. I have not eaten for hours, perhaps days. I cannot leave my post. If I do, another job suitor lurking behind the potted palm will steal Miss Buxton, my love.

10:00 A.M.
It's pouring outside. The receptionist says Miss Buxton has been called to an emergency meeting. No. It's another plot. If she goes to that meeting, she'll be riffed. I'll never be hired. We might never have our chance at immortality, at reinventing the general ledger. Give her this message. It's her only hope. My only hope. I scrawl: "Let's make your business our business. Still waiting, Jerry Slingsdorf."

10:30 A.M.

I read a *Guns and Ammo* magazine. I fidget. I
suck on an entire roll of breath mints. No word.
The guard stands at his post. My bladder is
ready to explode. Dare I leave? Will some other
job hunter who has been on a hundred interviews and sent out five-hundred resumés,
appear to take my place just as I'm relieving
myself? They're testing my will, my resolve.
Seeing if I'm in it just for the battle or for the
war. Nature can wait. It always has.

11:00 A.M.

The receptionist takes a call. Miss Buxton will
be just a few more minutes. She appreciates my
patience.

11:01 A.M.

I've been conned. Had. Three hours waiting in a
reception area. I fell for the job fake like a rook-
ie guarding Michael Jordan. I'm a man! A
human being! Do you hear me? I may not have
a job, but I have rights and dignity and credit
cards. I leave.

12:01 P.M.

The phone's ringing as I put the key in the door.
"Hello? Mr. Slingsdorf? This is Miss Candlehart
from Grigsby and Growley Accounting. I'm calling on behalf of Mr. Grigsby. Mr. Grigsby thinks
your resumé has panache. He's slotted you for a
2 P.M. interview Wednesday."

"Thank you. I'll be there." I hang up the
phone.

"Dad . . .er, Mr. Grigsby? I'm the man for
the job. I'll do my best to make you proud of
me."

Dreams

Frequently even your dreams will be tuned to the job-hunting channel. This can be disturbing, especially when your sleep is interrupted and you wake up screaming, "No, I will not describe my weaknesses unless you tell me yours first!"

Expect to dream that you are buck naked during an interview at least four times during the course of your job search. Do not be alarmed. This is healthy. Dreams act as a release for your anxieties. Continue to dream as you normally do—not that you have any choice.

Here are some of the more entertaining job-hunting dreams duly recorded by our staff.

Support Group Hell

One job-seeker dreamed about meeting some famous unemployed world leaders. "I'm in this job-hunting group with Mussolini, Genghis Khan, Marcos, Stalin, Nixon, and Millard Fillmore. I'm not sure why Fillmore's there, but he seems like an okay guy.

"Anyway, nobody seems to be listening to anybody else. Everybody's in denial. They've all got their scapegoat for being out of work. Mussolini says male pattern baldness was the cause of his demise. Marcos blames spoiled food as the reason he had to flee the presidential palace. Nixon mumbles, 'I'm no crook,' while he fumbles to locate the stop button on a tape recorder.

"After each person stands up to say, 'My name is _____ and I'm unemployed,' we check in with a progress report. Stalin says he's called every country in South America, with no luck. Genghis has been offered a part-time position in Iceland, but he can't bring his Mongol Horde. He has until Tuesday to decide. Now it's my turn, but I'm embarrassed because I wouldn't be much good at being a dictator, even for a small country like Belgium. I'm in the insurance business. That's when I wake up."

The Finger-in-the-ear Ploy

A man seeking work in medical equipment sales reports this dream: "I'm a final candidate for a top position. The problem is my prospective boss. She keeps her right index finger in her ear during our interview. When I ask her if I've got the job, she says, 'I'm sorry, I can't hear you, I've got my finger in my ear.' I never get the job."

Bowling Madness

An insurance salesman phoned this in: "It's my bowling night. Everything's fine until I realize the pins are actually the people I've interviewed with. Well, who cares? I've got a good game going. I'm down to the last frame and a chance for a score over 50, which I haven't had in weeks. There's one pin still standing—some guy who rejected me after five interviews. The ball comes up the chute. I look down to see the face of my girlfriend on the ball. I have to put my fingers in her nostrils and mouth to bowl. I roll a gutter ball."

"The Line"

Most job-hunters have a healthy distaste for the unemployment line and with good reason. The unemployment line is no pleasure palace. This much we know about it:

- ▼ You never get enough, but you keep coming back every two weeks anyway.

- ▼ It's more fun than cleaning the toilet, but less enjoyable than getting a root canal.

- ▼ You're getting paid about three dollars an hour to stand in line.

Yet here is also a place where you have something in common with everybody, which is not easy to find these days. You're in it together, this job-hunting fix. Think of your fellow standees as your wartime comrades in the battle to find employment. Remember that some of the best friendships come out of war.

Standing in the unemployment line may not excite you. But I recall the sage advice of my father, who said: "You make your own good time." He used to say that, of course, while we were stranded on the freeway with a flat tire.

To help you make your own good time while you wait for your check, here are some tips for your adventure in the unemployment line. These are simple, inexpensive ways to have fun, be productive, exercise, meet new people, pursue a hobby—heck, even make a few bucks.

▼ **Exercise** You want to be a lean and mean job-hunting machine, right? Here's where you start. This is a perfect place for aerobics. Instead of standing in place, bring your workout tape and burn fat while you do the job rap. Work up a sweat. This may help you get through the line quicker. Your fellow standees, realizing you need a shower, may permit you to go first.

Organize an athletic team with your fellow job-hunters. Put up flyers and challenge other offices to a bowling or baseball competition. Practice your pitching, tennis serve, or fly cast while you wait.

▼ **Practice interviewing** The unemployment line is a perfect place to practice your interview skills. Simply turn to your neighbor and say, "Tell me about yourself." Let the person ramble for a few minutes, then take turns answering requisite job interviewing questions. By day's end, you'll have met some new folks, talked about the person you're most interested in—yourself— and practiced an important job-hunting skill.

▼ **Party time** Think of the unemployment office as more than a place to pick up your check. It's also a social center, a pickup joint, a sort of clubhouse for the unemployed.

If you're having trouble finding a job, try your luck and skill at the age-old game of love. You might come up a winner. "Let's compare benefits," "There's no line at my place," "Come here often?" or "You have a great way of standing in line." These are a few time-proven, get-acquainted lines to help you get started.

Turn your job opportunity center into a movin' and groovin' party place. The unemployment line is a great place to dance. Bring one of your favorite tapes. Crank it up and form a conga line, a contra line, or simply move in place to some rap music.

▼ **Entrepreneurial unemployment** Let's face it. Your fellow job-hunters could maybe use a little extra cash. Am I right? And so could you, for that matter. Give your buddies a chance to double the size of their check. Organize a little poker game or black jack outside the unemployment office. (You're the dealer, of course.) Since this income is government-sponsored, you do not have to report your winnings.

▼ **Hygiene** There's no better place to practice personal hygiene than the unemployment line. There is much to do and you've got plenty of time to do it. So why not floss your teeth, clip your toenails, shave your five o'clock shadow, or apply makeup to your drab face? You need to look good for your upcoming interview, don't you?

By the time you reach the front, you could have given yourself a full facial, manicure, and pedicure. You may look like hell when you get in line, but by the time you receive your check, you're not only looking great, you're also feeling better because someone is handing you money. Psychologically, folks, this is good for you.

Help each other. Group hygiene activities help recreate a convivial office atmosphere. Apply blush to your friend's cheeks or comb your partner's hair.

Do remember to be neat. Since other people will be primping after you've finished, make sure to clean up your mess.

▼ **That's entertainment**   The unemployment office is one place that could use a little entertainment. Never have so many people stood in line for so long and been so unamused.

If you're a stand-up comedian, or have ever wanted to be, here's your opportunity.

Practice your instrument. Bring your Boogey Board or your Hacky Sack. Juggle.

Set up the popular Japanese karaoke, which allows you to sing to your favorite tunes. Invite others to crank out a few songs while they're in line. This is a great way to entertain as well as to relieve the stress of unemployment.

▼ **Group support**   There's strength in numbers. Hold hands and lead the line in a soulful rendition of "We Shall Be Employed" (sung to the tune of "We Shall Overcome").

We shall be employed.
We shall be employed.
We shall be employed, someday.
Oh, deep in my heart
I do believe
We shall find a job someday.

If Robert Frost had lost his job as a poet during modern times, he might have reworked his famous poem into this:

Stopping by an Unemployment Office on a Muggy Day

What line is this I think I know.
Where people move inch by inch, to and fro
I have resumés to send out; positions to check,
But miles to go before I collect.

My little son must think it weird
That the line is long; only one cashier.
He gives me a look.
Is there some mistake?
The only other sound's the sweep
Of shuffling feet and stomachache.

I have people to call; interviews to set,
But miles to go before I collect.

A voice concerned; to get my check.
The President says no help, sends regrets.
The line is long, slow and wet,
But I have miles to go before I collect.

It's been an hour, a day or more.
Still we haven't met our lady fore.
We need a shower, a bite, some sleep, a shave,
Another step ahead we take.

We'll get our due, we have no fear
Then we'll get the hell out of here.
The line is long, slow and wet.
But I have miles to go before I collect,
And miles to go before I collect.

Chapter Seven
The Domestic Front

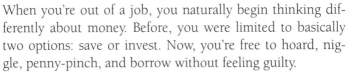

When you're out of a job, you naturally begin thinking differently about money. Before, you were limited to basically two options: save or invest. Now, you're free to hoard, niggle, penny-pinch, and borrow without feeling guilty.

The object of your money-saving tactics, of course, is to retain the same standard of living. To accomplish this, all you need to do is stop spending money.

You can always start clipping coupons with a vengeance, or switch to powdered milk; but you're missing the whole point. If you're going to have to trim expenses while you're in between jobs, why not have fun doing it? Make a game out of saving money. Do it with style, flair, and a sense of adventure.

Saving Money

Transportation

Whether you drive a car or use public transportation, this is an easy way to save money. Become a self-appointed public transit employee by wearing a conductor's uniform when you board the train or bus. Besides, it's always fun to punch people's tickets and tell them where to get off.

If you don't want to trade your car in for a moped, have others share their gasoline with you. Siphoning, popular during the energy crunch of the 1970s, is a viable alternative to beating the high prices at the pump.

But be polite about it. Remember—you are doing it for

a good cause—so you can afford to drive to your interview. Okay, so you have to shop, go to the ball game, play golf before that interview that hasn't been scheduled yet, but fair is fair. These people have jobs, and since they haven't offered to share their job with you, it's only fair they share their gasoline.

Print up flyers to put on windshields that say, "Thanks for giving me gas!" Also include your resumé and the sort of job you're looking for.

Vacations

You're probably thinking of giving up travel for a while. What for? There are people out there who are dying for you to come to their resort and stay a few days, have a free meal, and use all the facilities. These are called time shares. As an inducement for you to visit and buy a time share, these companies offer you free goodies.

Of course, you will have to listen to a canned talk for an hour or so, but after that you're home free. You may be able to cut the sales talk down to one minute by simply telling them you are not employed at the present time.

Utility Bills

This is a simple one. Move to Idaho. Already live in Idaho? No problem. Move to New York City for one month, pay the exorbitant gas bill, move back to Idaho, and see how much money you save. This is also a good way to see the country.

Communication

Postage stamps and the telephone are costs easily cut in half. Letters don't cost much money—it's those damned twenty-nine-cent stamps. Stamps. Who needs them? They don't taste good, anyway.

Why bother using them? Since the mail you send is so darned important, surely the receiving party will spend twenty-nine measly cents to see what you have to say.

Here's the simple solution. Where you formerly placed a stamp, simply write, "Postage will be paid by addressee." Do you think the credit card companies or your friends will refuse your payment just because it isn't stamped?

If they won't pay the postage, then you don't need friends or businesses that are so cheap they won't put out some measly change for you. Write 'em off.

Monthly telephone service is a given; the problem is those damned long-distance telephone calls they insist on billing you for.

Here is where your nearby hotel can provide a service even if you're not staying there. Simply wander over, and pick up the house phone. This is meant for anyone who lives in a house. Apartments are okay, too.

Charge your call to a randomly picked hotel room in Europe. With any luck, the room will be vacant. You can be sure the occupant won't pay the bill, but the hotel gladly considers it part of the cost of doing business.

Food and Laundry

Hotels are also good for a quick snack, sometimes a whole meal. Check the hotel's marquee for business meetings and arrive when the meal begins. Worried about not knowing what's going on? No problem. Respond to business questions with, "I never talk business during lunch, (dinner)." Then bring up your own favorite topic for discussion.

Roadkills. They're not for everybody. They may be for you. Won't your family be surprised when you bring home exotic cuts of meat like venison, bear, moose, rabbit? And it's all free! Your car and you work together to "bring home the bacon."

Thanks to the gang at the Department of Highways for posting the signs "Deer Crossing" or "Watch for Moose." You can park your car nearby and wait for your prey. Happy hunting!

Yes, you can save money even at the laundromat. You've heard of car pooling. Try clothes-pooling. Since somebody is already washing his or her clothes, why not go along for the ride? Simply combine your wash with other loads "in-progress."

Here's how you do it: As you throw clothes into your laundry mate's washer, ask, "Mind if I join you?" or "Since we're both doing whites . . ."

For the less bold, the answer is to throw your clothes in the washer the moment the person leaves the laundromat to do errands. Remove your clothes before they return. Use the same technique for drying.

Be forewarned. At some point you will probably get caught. "The next round is on me" is an excellent comeback to "What the hell do you think you're doing?"

Night Life

Just because you're a little short on cash is no reason to stop going to the movies, the theater, or art exhibitions. In fact, these are great places to make some extra money.

Volunteer to usher at your local theater. You get in free to see the play. But there's no reason to leave empty-handed. If you've ever been to Europe, you know that ushers expect a tip for showing you to your seat.

Practice your haughty French accent, and carry a small duster with you, which you will use to gently whisk away nonexistent matter. When you hand your customers their programs, announce loudly enough for others to hear, "It is my pleasure to serve you. If you need anything, my name is Jacques."

Here is where you must walk a fine line between groveling and sticking to your guns. At this point, do not move. Look your customers in the eye, and put your hand, palm open, within in full view of your clients. If they don't get the idea, turn away slightly and hold your hand behind you so that it is perpendicular to your torso. Expect to feel the coolness of quarters or the finer texture of dollar bills in your hand.

Art openings are a great way to eat, earn extra cash, and become cultured at the same time. Want to be a trendsetter? Be the first in the art world to charge an admission fee.

Dress in black and white. Position yourself at the door. Then proposition each person for a few dollars to defray costs. "We're asking for a small donation to ensure that the artist can continue to produce the work so important to us all." This works well. Since many of the attendees will be friends or admirers of the artist, they'll be hard-pressed to say no.

And you're not really lying, because you didn't say what artist they're contributing to. The artist, of course, is you. You're artistic. We all are. There's an art to everything. You are presently involved in the fine art of looking for a job, for example.

The important thing is that everybody goes home happy. The artist has had a day in the spotlight; the crowd is happy because they think they've contributed to the emergence of the next Picasso; and you go home with fifty bucks, maybe a hundred on a good night. If you're really entrepreneurial, you can work several art openings in a single night.

Oh yes, art openings always have food and wine. Don't forget to avail yourself of the drinks and hors d'oeuvres. You've earned it.

National Association for the Advancement of Unemployed People

Above all, join the National Association for the Advancement of Unemployed People. Never heard of it? Consider yourself a charter member by printing yourself an identification card. You decide on the privileges, and put them on your card.

Some good ones are "Two dinners for the price of one" at popular restaurants. Or the catch-all, "Seventy percent off everything in stock."

If you're questioned, say, "If you ever lose your job, you can count on me to honor your membership."

National Association for the Advancement of Unemployed People

"Looking for Work Is Job One"

(Name)

is a member in good standing with the NAAUP and has agreed to abide by all regulations of the organization. When this card is shown, the member must be accorded all privileges:

- Free second helpings
- Free gas on weekends
- Free psychiatric counseling
- Free box seats

- Free tuition
- Free admission
- Free "safe" sex
- 70% discount on luxuries

Scott Badler
Executive Director

Unemployed Sex

Being unemployed changes sex. For many, sex is an integral part of the job-hunting equation. Consider the following:

$$\text{Sex} = \frac{\text{Networking}^2}{\text{Cover Letters}}$$

Although some unmarried job-hunters say their sex lives improve—because the act is so rarely performed, it is a thrill to actually engage in the act—finding a sexual partner is as difficult as beating the bushes for a job.

In fact, many job-hunters postulate that sex and job-hunting are interchangeable: You meet a lot of people who say no, but sooner or later somebody says, "Okay, I would like to have sex/have work with you." This is a happy day, for now you will have a regular sex/work schedule with full benefits.

In the beginning, the sex/work goes really well. You do it almost every day. You're excited about doing it. You think about it all the time, even when you're not doing it. You even perform it overtime. You have sex/work lunches. You consider yourself creative at your sex/work and are proud of it. You brag to your friends of your accomplishments. Your identify yourself through your sex/work. When somebody asks, "How's sex/work going?" you say, "I really enjoy it, it's a great bunch of people I have sex/work with. Really nice. It's like one big sex/work family."

When your sex/work is finished, you're exhausted, but you don't mind because you know you did a good job. Shortly thereafter, you're knocking at the door, requesting more sex/work. You are passionate about your sex/work.

Unfortunately, some people become obsessed. All they want to do is have sex/work. These are called sex/workaholics. They are boring people. Their common complaint is "All I ever do is sex/work."

Compatibility is a thorny problem for people involved in sex/work relationships. Half, or in some cases, a third, of sex/work partnerships may want sex/work all the time. This may result in one person saying, "All you want me for is my sex/work." This may be true, especially if one person has been blessed with particularly noteworthy sex/work attributes.

To some people, sex/work is an unpleasant task, one of life's dreaded activities. "It pays the bills." But to get through it, sex/workers drink a lot of coffee, finish before everyone else, or fake it.

Be forewarned that during your sex/work lives, you can expect many changes. The average sex/worker switches partners an average of six times during a lifetime. Of course, our sex/work habits change during our lifetime. As we get older, our desire for sex/work gradually diminishes. When we are young, performing sex/work almost every day is quite common. However, at some point, many people stop having sex/work. They have no more interest, perhaps, because it takes so long to complete a single sex/work task. This is known as retirement. It is supposed to be a happy time, full of relaxation, free from the demands of sex/work.

Reassessment of your sex/work schedule is necessary when the person you're having sex/work with becomes dissatisfied with your performance. You may be told the sex/work is over. Or you may be shifted to a new office where you are forced to have sex/work with strangers. This is quite an adjustment. After all, for several years you went to the same place for sex/work. These new people do it in weird ways, perhaps performing the sex/work in groups when you are used to doing it alone or with one other person. Their style may be to have endless conjugal meetings that last forever and wind up with nobody feeling satisfied.

Sex/work may terminate because of poor communication between you and your partner. You find it difficult to talk and express your needs. So you rely on memos. This makes it hard to have satisfactory sex/work. You never know what your sex/work partner really wants, so you both feel frustrated.

Sex/work may be halted when some young go-getter does the job better than you. This is a blow to one's self-esteem, no doubt about it. Now you're out on the street again looking for sex/work. When this happens, always remember that somebody else out there thinks you're pretty good at sex/work and will give you a golden opportunity to prove it.

Sometimes your sex/work relocates to another city. Should you go? Now you have to ask yourself questions like these: Was it that good? Will I be able to find sex/work where I currently live?

It is always a good idea to evaluate your present sex/work situation at various intervals. Asking yourself these questions will help you decide whether you need a change:

1. Am I bored with my sex/work?
2. Would the addition of another person help my sex/work?
3. Should I look for an additional part-time sex/work position?
4. Am I getting paid enough for my sex/work?
5. Do I always have a headache when it comes time to have sex/work?

At some point, you may be fired, or quit; the result means a return to "looking for a job/having sex with your-self." But don't despair. Sooner or later, someone else will offer you a position in middle management sex/work. "Hey, join us," your prospective employer will say. "We want to have sex/work with you."

Some final thoughts on work/sex:

- ▲ Sometimes you're on top, other times, the bottom.
- ▲ The best sex/work is stimulating and challenging.
- ▲ Be creative. Think of new ways to perform your sex/work.
- ▲ Never quit before you have lined up other sex/work.

Chasing Away Those Job-hunting Blues

Made 287 calls today without one call back? Feeling a tad discouraged? Take a few seconds to chase away those blues. Try these seven helpful hints:

1. Go to the local elementary school. Wipe out the seventh graders in tetherball.
2. Reserve the most expensive restaurant or hotel. This is guaranteed to make you feel better. Make sure to cancel later.
3. Tell an employer you accepted another job for ten times what they were offering.
4. Challenge any senior citizen at the nursing home to a hundred-yard dash.
5. Do a primal job scream in the unemployment office.
6. Hijack a limousine and cruise the town.
7. Place a help-wanted ad, then reject the applicants.

Chapter Eight
Looking for Work: An Autopsy

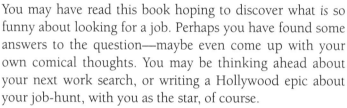

You may have read this book hoping to discover what *is* so funny about looking for a job. Perhaps you have found some answers to the question—maybe even come up with your own comical thoughts. You may be thinking ahead about your next work search, or writing a Hollywood epic about your job-hunt, with you as the star, of course.

On the other hand, you may be saying to yourself and to others on the bus, "There is nothing funny about looking for a job." That's fine, too. This may mean you're ready to stop looking for a job and go into business on your own. Going into business on your own can be funny, also. But that's another story.

Perhaps you got a job halfway through reading this book. That's great! I hereby take full credit for your success and will accept a commission based on 50 percent of your salary per month times ten, payable immediately.

Maybe you're a reader who isn't looking for work at the moment but who wanted to see what was so funny about looking for a job. This is excellent thinking. You are ahead of the game and can expect to have many successful years of job-hunting with this positive, "plan-ahead" attitude.

Or, you may be a human resources representative of a Fortune 500 company, anxious to find out what today's pavement-pounders are up to. You bought this book hoping to find new ways to discourage job-hunters. If this is you, you are in direct violation of the Human Resources Act of

1943, which forbids people employed in personnel to read anything other than resumés. As your punishment, you must now stand in an unemployment line for five hours a week and write letters of apology to all job-seekers you have thus far rejected.

Others may be asking themselves this question: Was it worth spending my time reading this book when I could have been faxing resumés or making cold calls? This is a good question for which there is no easy or correct answer. But maybe it's hindsight. And if you're hindsighted, maybe it's time for a new prescription.

Now that you've learned about the inherent humor of looking for work, do not think this assures you of your dream job. To be sure, nobody ever laughed their way to a job. But it is also true that nobody ever got one by crying a river. With one exception. Me. I was at my second interview when I asked my prospective employer if he wanted anything else. He said, "How about 'Cry Me a River,' by Joe Cocker?" But that was an exception. Most often employers ask for "Stairway to Heaven" or "Light My Fire."

In any event, you now realize that anything goes when you're job-hunting. There are no *Roberts Rules of Looking for Work* or *Chicago Manual of Style for Job-hunting*. Anything you do to find a job is legal under the Job-hunting Act of 1888, which guarantees you the right to "do weird stuff in order to find gainful work." You can't be arrested for what you do in the course of a job hunt, which is too bad because (1) being arrested gets you out of the house and (2) your cell mates may have some hot job leads.

You must have figured out by now that looking for work is a crazy enterprise. One never knows where it will lead. One day you find yourself on a wild safari hunting down a lead in Africa, and the next day you're practicing your interviewing skills on your neghbor's two-year old son. (a close approximation to the real thing).

Nevertheless, this is an exciting time for job-hunting, and you are at the forefront. You are the innovator, the salivater, the hyperventilater. But even though the field is going through vast changes, job-hunters will never lose their place in society. As long as the human race needs something to do between the hours of nine and five, the worthy endeavor of job-hunting, like the cockroach, will survive. (Find me a cockroach who's not working nights, and I'll show you a cockroach with time on its hands.)

And now for some final words of empowerment. A call for job-hunters to unite, to take back the country from those who have their own cubicles, plenty of paper clips, and access to the copy machine. Millions strong, we constitute an enormous voting bloc. It is time we came "out of the unemployment line" and said, "I am unemployed and proud of it," or something to that effect.

Ever since disgruntled job-seeker Charles Guiteau assassinated President James Garfield, we job-hunters have become society's whipping boys/girls. That is why we are made to stand for hours in the unemployment line. The time is ripe to make our voices heard, to use our strength-in-numbers, to form lobbies, to march on Washington, to demand two-for-one movie discounts. Plans call for a National Job-hunting Day (tentatively scheduled for the day before Labor Day) to honor the millions who have given a portion of their lives to haranguing human resources personnel.

Even as we speak, architects are busy drawing up plans for a National Museum of Job-hunting. An entire floor is to be set aside for the Study of Networking, and the "interactive" exhibit will include practice time for museum visitors. A job-hunting amusement park is under consideration for Poughkeepsie, New York. Sure to be a hit there is Personnel Workers in the Sea of Cortez, which makes riders navigate their resumés past blood-thirsty human resource personnel to get them on the desks of hiring managers. Failure means a dunking in the cold, deep, circular file cabinet.

Some final advice: Life doesn't stop while you're looking for a job. If it does, check your batteries. Every once in a while when things seem tough, when you can't even get your mother to return your phone call, take a good look in the mirror and say, "Somebody out there is going to hire me."

Then peel off your business suit and go to the beach! You deserve it.

Best of luck.